Frank C. Laubach

CHRIST LIVETH IN ME

and

GAME WITH MINUTES

FLEMING H. REVELL COMPANY

Scriptures quoted in this book are from various versions, and from free translations by the author, including his own *Inspired Letters in Clearest English,* copyright 1956 by Thomas Nelson & Sons; and the *Revised Standard Version of the Bible,* copyright 1946 and 1952 by the Division of Christian Education of the National Council of Churches.

Acknowledgment is made for use of material from *Songs from the Slums* by Toyohiko Kagawa. Copyright 1935 by Whitmore & Smith. By permission of Abingdon Press.

The Poem, "The Postern Gate," by Walter Rauschenbusch was originally printed by the author on a Christmas card. See D. R. Sharpe, *Walter Rauschenbusch,* p. 451, published by The Macmillan Company, 1942.

CHRIST LIVETH IN ME

Christ Liveth in Me

I am writing this on the day before Christmas. We have just sung:

> O holy child of Bethlehem,
> Descend to us, we pray,
> Cast out our sin, and enter in—
> Be born in us today.

And we sang:

> O come to my heart, Lord Jesus,
> There is room in my heart for Thee.

And we sang:

> He lives, He lives! Christ Jesus lives today!
> You ask me how I know He lives,
> He lives within my heart.

And we sang:

> O what a salvation this
> That Christ liveth in me!

And we sang:

> Come into my heart, Lord Jesus;
> Come in today, come in to stay,
> Come into my heart, Lord Jesus.

And we sang:

> Where meek souls will receive Him, still
> The dear Christ enters in.

J. B. Phillips says that these songs which many of us sing at Christmas about the Christ Child entering us express the profoundest experience of the Christian religion. If this is *really* true, if Christ *does* come into us—really—and if He stays, that *is* indeed the most marvelous experience of our lives. Nothing else in the world is so important.

> Though Christ a thousand times
> In Bethlehem be born,
> If He's not born in thee
> Thy soul is still forlorn.
> —Angelus Silesius

Does anybody ever have Christ living in him *all the time?* Yes, millions have testified that they do. Let us start with St. Paul. In Galatians 2:20, he said, "Christ liveth in me." Paul said it at least sixty-six other times, many different ways. Paul did not speak about himself alone. He meant that Christ may be in all of us. He said, "Our bodies are meant for Christ to dwell in." He begged his friends to "Take Christ into your heart." He said, "I pray that he may live in your hearts." Paul also said, "Do you not understand that Christ lives in you?" He wrote to the Christians in Philippi, "Christ is in your hearts." Paul goes so far as to say that our very eternal life depends upon Christ being in us now: "Christ in you is your hope of glory."

WHERE IS GOD'S RIGHT HAND?

Many people believe that Christ is not here in this world, but that He sits far off in heaven at the right hand of God, and that it is the *Holy Spirit* that comes into our hearts. What shall we believe about this? Jesus

Himself said, "I will not leave you comfortless; I will come again. The world will not see me, but you will see me."

How can Christ be at God's right hand and yet be *in us? Where is God's right hand?* Is God beyond the stars? It takes the light several billions of years to come from the most distant galaxies. God's throne reaches beyond those stars. Yet God is here also. He is everywhere. He is a big God. This whole universe is His throne. He is so big that He fills the entire universe. His throne is vastly larger than we can realize. But the point at which we can touch Him is *here,* for this is part of His throne. Paul told the Athenians: "He is not far from any one of us, for in him we live and move and have our being." The majestic 139th Psalm says this:

> If I ascend up into heaven, thou art there;
> If I make my bed in hell, behold, thou art there;
> If I take the wings of the morning, and dwell in the
>   uttermost parts of the sea,
> Even there shall thy hand lead me, and thy right
>   hand shall hold me. . . .
> Thou hast beset me behind and before, and laid
>   thine hand upon me. . . .

God's arm is holding you! So if Jesus "took his seat at God's right hand" that brings Jesus very close. He too is holding you!

But Paul goes even closer than that. He says, "Christ is *in your very heart!*"

THE THREE ARE ONE

The Comforter, the Holy Spirit, is in our hearts, but Jesus Christ is also there. Whatever the Trinity is, it is never divided, one-third here and two-thirds far off. Never! The Three are always inseparable. If you wish to confirm this, look at Acts 16. In verse 6, Luke says that Paul and his comrades were "forbidden by the Holy Spirit to speak the word in Asia." The next verse, Acts 16:7, says, "they attempted to go into Bithynia, but the *Spirit of Jesus* did not allow them." In Acts 16:10 Luke says, "We went to Macedonia concluding that God had called us to preach there." There is the whole Trinity in those three verses telling Paul what to do! Did one Person of the Trinity speak at one time, another at another time? Of course not! The Spirit of Jesus *is* the Holy Spirit; it is the "Holy Spirit of Jesus." "I and the Father are *one*"—they are one and inseparable: The Father is in the Son, the Son in the Father—all the time.

If the Holy Spirit is in you, the Spirit of Jesus is in you and the Father is in you. Paul says this over and over. "In Christ the whole of God dwells." "*God's own Spirit* is what you have received." "God's Spirit makes his home in *you*." "God's Spirit makes his home in our heart." "We have shared the very thoughts of God." "The Holy Spirit comes from God and dwells in you." "Your body is the temple of the Holy Spirit." "He poured his Holy Spirit into our hearts." "We have received God's Spirit." "I pray that you may be completely filled with God." That is what Jesus says in John 17:21, 26, when He prays that: "even as thou, Father, art in me, and I in thee, that they also may be in us . . . and . . . that the love with which thou hast loved me may be in them, and I in them." Here we see what Paul calls "the secret truth which God hid for ages, but revealed to us through Jesus Christ." The astounding secret is that the inseparable Trinity wants to bring you into itself, you in the Trinity (Father—Son—Spirit) and the Trinity in you.

7

So Paul says, "Your life is hid with Christ in God" (Colossians 3:3).

So you may speak to Him with any title that helps you most to feel His inner presence. You may say, "Jesus," or "Christ," or "Jesus Christ," or "Holy Spirit," or "God," or "Father," or "Eternal Spirit," or "Dear Jesus." Under whichever name, Christ and the Father are here with you—are *in you!* As Tennyson has said:

> Speak to Him, thou, for He hears, and Spirit with
> Spirit can meet—
> Closer is He than breathing, and nearer than hands
> and feet.

THE ASTOUNDING PLAN OF JESUS

Thus far we have been quoting from Paul, but now let us ask, What does Jesus Himself say about living in us? He says the most astounding thing! In John 6:51, 53, Jesus says that He came down to earth to be *eaten!* "I am the living bread which came down from heaven; if any one eats of this bread, he will live forever; and the bread which I shall give for the life of the world is my flesh." "Truly I say to you, unless you eat the flesh of the Son of man and drink his blood, you have no life in you; he who eats my flesh and drinks my blood has eternal life. . . . For my flesh is food indeed, and my blood is drink indeed." "He who eats my flesh and drinks my blood . . . *I [abide] in him.*"

Many of His disciples said, "This is a hard saying; who can listen to it?" But Jesus replied: "The words that I have spoken to you are about spirit and life. . . . It is the spirit that gives life, the flesh is of no avail."

This is precisely what Jesus said again at the Last

8

Supper. It is quoted in four different places in the New Testament—Matthew, Mark, Luke, and Paul's First Letter to the Corinthians. "He took bread, and blessed, and broke it, and gave it to them, and said, Take; *this is my body.* And he took a cup and when he had given thanks he gave it to them and they all drank of it. And he said to them, *This is my blood . . .* which is poured out for many" (Mark 14:22-24). The moment you invite Him in with the bread and wine, He enters your soul. That act of receiving Him is the invitation for His Spirit to join our spirit.

The Lord's Supper is the central ritual of the Christian church today. It means a wide variety of things to those who partake of it, but it always opens every heart in loving receptivity to Christ, which is exactly what He desired.

The wonderful ex-cannibal Christians of the Pacific Islands understand this meaning of the Lord's Supper better than we do. The cannibals do not eat you because they are hungry for your *flesh.* They eat you because they admire you. It is your virtues they want. They eat your flesh to get your *strength,* or your *keen mind,* or your *good looks,* or your *leadership* or your *personality.* They eat your *flesh* to get your *spirit.* It is a compliment to be eaten by cannibals!

The only person in history who ever asked people to eat him was Jesus. He loved parables and He used this, the most startling and even shocking illustration He could find. That is the deepest meaning of the cross. On the cross His flesh was offered to us and His blood was poured out for us, so that we might eat and drink *His Spirit* and so that His Spirit might pour through our bodies, and His blood mingle with our blood, going to the tips of our fingers in arteries and capillaries.

9

HOW WE ARE BORN AGAIN

If Jesus were telling parables today, He would use another illustration. He would tell how the male cell penetrates the female cell at the time of conception. He would tell how the chromosomes rearrange themselves in an amazing manner, and a new creature is conceived. He did say that in substance in His conversation with Nicodemus, when He said: "Unless one is born anew he cannot see the kingdom of God." "Unless one is born of . . . the Spirit, he cannot enter the kingdom of God." When a male cell and a female cell unite, the new child has the natures of father and mother in him. So when God's Spirit penetrates our spirit, the "new creature" which is born partakes of the nature of God and of us—we are then both human and divine. That new Eternal Spirit of God, joined with your spirit, makes you eternal! That is how "mortality puts on immortality." In Colossians 3:3 Paul says: "For you died, and your life now is hid with Christ in God. . . . When He comes, you will be seen with Him in glory." In Galatians 4:19 Paul says: "I am suffering a mother's birth pangs . . . until Christ be formed in your hearts."

HE COMES IN *IF* . . .

Why is not Christ in all our hearts all the time? He does not come into our hearts unless we invite Him in. He says: "Behold, I stand at the door and knock; if any one hears my voice and opens the door, I will come in. . . ." But there is one condition on which He will come in. Paul said: "Do you not understand that Christ lives in you *if* . . . ?" There is an "if." Many people who read these pages will say, "I have no experience of Christ inside me." They are right. He is not inside because they have not obeyed the "if."

What is that "if"? I John 4:12 says it very plainly. "If we love one another, God abides in us." "God is love, and he who abides in love abides in God, and God abides in him" (4:16). "He who does not love does not know God; for God is love" (4:8). I John 3:17 says, "If any one has the world's goods and sees his brother in need, yet closes his heart against him, how does God's love abide in him?" So Love is one "if."

But there is another "if." I John 3:24 says: "All who keep his commandments abide in him, and he in them." Keeping these commandments is the other "if."

This is illustrated by Roland Brown's vision. He thought he could see his own mind, which was like a vast hall. Roland heard a knock at the front door of his mind and opened the door. There stood Jesus! Roland cried in joy: "Come in, Jesus, I am so glad to see you!" But Jesus shook His head and said: "No. I cannot come in unless you permit me to sit on the throne of your mind. I must be Lord and King and Master, or I cannot come in at all." Roland replied: "Come and occupy the throne and be my King and Lord and Master." Then in Roland's vision, Jesus entered and took the throne. When Allan Hunter heard Roland Brown tell that story, Allan said: "That is authentic! Jesus could never enter and permit us to rule Him. He would be ruined if He shrank to our size, and shared our petty prejudices and connived in our selfish purposes." If He enters us it is not to help us with our little aims, but to make our aims bigger; to transform us into His likeness and to enlarge our goals to His size. He comes to be king—and we must surrender our wills to Him.

11

THE EVERLASTING OBEDIENCE OF JESUS

What Jesus demands of us corresponds to His own relationship with His Father. He repeats this forty-nine times in John's Gospel, as though to make it unmistakable and unforgettable. "I do only what I see the Father do—what I hear from the Father—what he tells me to do." The reason the Father can trust the Son with all the worlds and for all eternity is because the Son is utterly dependable, incessantly dependable, in every tiny detail, under every temptation or trial. We see this: 1) when the devil tempted Jesus, and 2) again in Gethsemane, and 3) in His final trial, and 4) on the cross. "Utter obedience" is the strait gate and the narrow way that leads to life "and few there be that find it." That seems to be true even today of most of the human race. They do not find this narrow way of total obedience. If we found it we should be as good as Jesus—but not quite, for He has a history which we can never match. Never at any moment of any hour of any century in ten billion years has He failed to obey the Father. That no other person can say.

PREPARING US TO JOIN THE DIVINE FAMILY

The Father plans to invite us to join His divine family, but we cannot join it unless we enter this family with the same perfect surrender of our wills to God's will as Jesus has. The Kingdom is an absolute monarchy; it is not a "democracy." If we are like Jesus we stand face to face before God every moment and listen for His every order. As He issues commands, we carry them out. We are God's perfect servants.

Yet He does not stand over us with a whip and make us

12

do the work alone. In fact He does more of the work always than we do. We are his "yoke fellows" like two oxen or horses hitched together. God loves to work *with* us, because when we and He work together *we* are growing into fitness for joining His eternal divine family. So Paul says: "We are fellow workers together with him." God *could* have made the world perfect without our aid, but we would then have lost this most marvelous of all opportunities to *grow like Him by working with Him*. In James Russell Lowell's words:

> Who gives himself with his alms feeds three,
> Himself, his hungering neighbor, and Me.

WORSHIP OF A FALSE FREEDOM

Americans talk about our "freedom" as though freedom were our religion. We call America the "land of the free." But we are not free from God. Our ancestors came to America to be free from men so that they could have but *one Master*, God. They could not serve two masters. Now we falsely assume we need not obey *any* master, not even God.

But when one thinks deeply, he sees how foolish we are. We see this truth when we think of "the laws of nature." There is no freedom in this universe except perfect obedience to the laws of the universe. Science seeks to know how the universe behaves, because only by knowing her ways can we know how we must obey. Perfect obedience gives us more "freedom," not *from* laws, but through *obeying* laws. Those who say "knowledge is power" are half wrong. The truth is that knowledge plus obedience to Nature's laws is power.

13

FALSE EDUCATION

In America we have confused our conception of political freedom with our religion. The so-called "new education" does not tell a child that he must obey every whisper of God, for in the public schools God must not be taught. The "new education" encourages a child to obey the whispers of his own impulses, not God's whisper. Many children now try to be free from God and men and law. They obey their whims. This is one of the reasons for juvenile delinquency. That kind of "new education" is not the doorway into the Kingdom of God; it is the doorway to prison and to hell. Nobody can enter the Kingdom of God—or even more abundant life—who tries to be free from God.

THE STARK DEMANDS OF JESUS

Jesus made His demand for complete surrender as clear as words could make it: "Not every one who says to me, 'Lord, Lord,' shall enter the kingdom of heaven, but he who does the will of my Father who is in heaven" (Matthew 7:21). "He who does not give up all he has and follow me, cannot be my disciple." "You are my friends if you do whatsoever I command you." "If a man loves me, he will keep my word, and my Father will love him, and we will come to him and make our home with him" (John 14:23). "If any man would come after me let him deny himself and take up his cross and follow me" (Matthew 16:24).

OUR WILLS MUST BE BORN AGAIN

This stark demand could drive us to dismay, for we know how easily we forget and disobey God, and how frequently we turn our backs on God to do our own will. The sin of Adam and Eve is still here to plague us all. We might *promise* God that we would not disobey Him, but we know that we would break that promise. The wayward mind and deed which we inherited from our ancestor Adam wants to sin, and it cannot keep the law.

That is the reason the Law of the Old Testament could not save us. We inherited the perverse nature of Adam, and are too weak to obey the law.

God has no illusion about that—"he knoweth that we are dust" and that our disposition is to sin. We do not approach Him because we are good, but because we need Him. We need to have Him inside to make our weakness strong and our bad nature good. We invite Him in, promising to *try,* but knowing that we are too weak to *succeed* without His aid. We count on Him inside to give us the power to do God's will which we do not have unless He gives us that power.

The alcoholic or drug addict whom Christ sets free from these habits understands this. He knows that his *will* must be "born again." The desire to drink or to use drugs is what Jesus takes away; and this desire stays away as long as the alcoholic keeps Christ in his life. But the moment the alcoholic leaves Christ outside the door and tries to go alone, the desire returns irresistibly and he falls again. Christ within him is his only strength.

We come to Him confessing our unworthiness and saying:

> Just as I am, without one plea,
> But that Thy blood was shed for me,

15

And that Thou biddest me come to Thee,
O Lamb of God, I come, I come.

Just as I am, poor, wretched, blind;
Sight, riches, healing of the mind,
Yea, all I need, in Thee to find,
O Lamb of God, I come, I come.

CHRIST PURSUES US

We cannot even come to Christ without His help. So
He comes to us! In fact, He pursues us. That tremendous
poem, "The Hound of Heaven," reveals this divine pur-
suing Lover as no other poem ever did. Christ pursues
us every hour until He gets us.

In the Old Testament, the prophet Hosea took his
wicked, wayward, adulterous wife back to his bosom and
made her love him so much that she lost her desire for
other men. That is what Christ does. He drives out the
desire for sin with "the expulsive power of a greater
affection." Jesus, like Hosea, pursues us, never giving us
up, day after day, year after year, until at last some day
when we are at the bottom and hopeless and helplessly
reaching out for help, He takes us to His arms.

If we had enough sensitivity for what is really noble,
this realization that Christ pursues us would break our
hearts. "O Christ, have you really followed me all the
way down to this sin? Did you follow me through all this
disgusting filth and pettiness and selfishness? Now here
at the bottom of this pit you have found me!"

O Jesus, Thou art standing
Outside the fast-closed door,
In lowly patience waiting
To pass the threshold o'er:

16

Shame on us, Christian brothers,
His name and sign who bear,
O shame, thrice shame upon us,
To keep Him standing there!

O Jesus, Thou art knocking;
And lo, that hand is scarred,
And thorns Thy brow encircle,
And tears Thy face have marred;
O love that passeth knowledge,
So patiently to wait!
O sin that hath no equal,
So fast to bar the gate!

So when we invite this "Stranger at the Door" to come in, we confess in shame: "It is a dirty and disorderly house, but it is yours to change as you will." And in He comes eagerly, on that basis, as the new Master of the house, and we remain with Him as His servant.

HE PUTS STEEL INTO WEAK WILLS

We offer Him our weak wills so He can put steel into them and make them strong.

Laid on thine altar, O my Lord divine,
Accept my will this day, for Jesus' sake.
. . . Here within my trembling hand I bring
This will of mine, a thing which seemeth small,
But thou alone, O Lord, canst understand
That when I bring my will, I bring my all.

Our weak, wayward, wobbling *will* is the first thing our Senior Partner makes over when we invite Him in. He makes it strong.

Jesus said that it is not the deed that is the sin; it is

the will to do evil that is wicked. "They said of old times, thou shalt not kill, but I say *thou shalt not hate*." "They said, do not commit adultery, but I say do not lust." Deep in the subconscious desires the indwelling Christ cleans house when He moves in.

Our judges and our police punish only the outward acts, but the judgment of God is against the sinful *will*. This will to sin is what we surrender when Christ comes in. He replaces it with a will for good. The fascination for sin is taken away.

Beginning at Romans 7:12, Paul says perfectly what we all experience. "I find it to be the law of my nature that when I want to do right, evil is still with me. For I delight in the law of God down in my soul. But in my body is another law at war with the law of my mind. That law in my body makes me a prisoner of sin which is in my body. Unhappy man that I am, who will set me free from this body bound to death? Thanks be to God who sent Jesus Christ our Lord. He has set me free."

When Christ's Spirit enters and mingles with our spirit, the reborn soul has a *reborn will*. It is not a *new birth* unless it is a *new will*. This new will loves to do the will of God, just as Christ loves to do God's will. Christ's nature transforms ours. We no longer want to sin. The old son of Adam could not obey; the new son of God loves to obey. I John 3:9 says: "Anyone who is born again is a child of God and does not commit sin. God's nature is in him. He cannot live in sin because he is born again and he is God's child."

THE COROLLARIES

If you studied geometry in your high school days, you remember that below each proposition which we proved there were "corollaries." We learned to prove that the three angles inside a triangle are equal to a straight line. Then below that proposition we have five or six corollaries.

If we accept the proposition that "Christ liveth in me," what are the "corollaries"? They are amazing!

First Corollary: We Dwell in the Same House

From the moment He enters, we dwell together for the rest of our lives in this same house. When I shut my eyelids I have pulled down the curtains and there are only two of us left in the house. Nobody else is in my heart or mind, nobody else walks through my veins and arteries and nerves, nobody else but Jesus. It is His house and it is mine—it is ours! "And so we dwell together, my Lord and I."

The nuns in convents aspire to become the brides of Christ. The most astonishing spiritual biography in the world is perhaps that of Santa Teresa in her "Interior Castle," the story of her betrothal and inner marriage with Christ. We men find that marriage idea unnatural to us. But we can accept Him as our Senior Partner.

So when His will and ours blend into one, He and we live in our bodies, reach out through our hands, look out through our eyes, speak out through our tongues, and walk out with our feet. We do it hands joined to hands, like two lovers. In our bodies today He continues to save the world, the task which He began as a Child in Bethlehem. We help Him with our witness and our lives. He knocks at other hearts, and the knuckles with which He knocks are our knuckles! He stands at the door and knocks at every heart. The voice outside the other hearts with which He calls is *our voice* and *His*.

Second Corollary: We Experience Partnership in a World Enterprise

When He enters, we change our business. We put *His* shingle up, and it is "The Kingdom of God." As His junior partner, my business is to offer my mind to Him, my hands to Him, every fiber of my body to Him, to work for His Kingdom. Right now while typing these words, I have been saying: "Here is your body, Partner. Here are your fingers. Here is your brain. Take me and think and write what you will about your plan. Help me that I may instantly and totally respond as you dictate, for I am your typist, your stenographer."

Third Corollary: This Partnership Can Do Infinitely More

When we thus totally and without hindrance let Him possess us, He can do something for the world that can never be done through us until we are His, and wholly His to be used. No one ever saw this more perfectly or said it more beautifully than Toyohiko Kagawa:

> . . . today
> A wonderful thought
> In the dawn was given,
>
> *   *   *
>
> And the thought
> Was this:
> That a secret plan
> Is hid in my hand;
> That my hand is big,
> Big,
> Because of this plan.
>
> That God,
> Who dwells in my hand,

Knows this secret plan
Of the things He will do for the world
Using my hand!

What a wonderful thing Kagawa did for the world! Kagawa let God use his hand to write several hundred Christian books. Japan is 98.4 per cent literate, and millions of copies of these were sold to the entire Japanese nation. Today Japan is on the way to becoming a Christian nation, because God, who lived in Kagawa's hand, with that hand was able to reach into the minds of thousands of the people of Japan and plant God's thoughts there.

I do not for an instant doubt that if we let God have His own way, all of us would also discover that our hands and tongues and eyes are big, "big because of the plan," because God who dwells in them has a secret plan of the things He will do for the world, using their hands and bodies and eyes and minds.

The Risen Lord is working. We open our doors, He enters and rolls up His sleeves and goes on with His work —through us! This is what Paul meant when he said: "God working through us is able to do unutterably more. . . ." Unutterably more than we ever could do alone, and more than He could do without us. We need God, and *God needs us*.

You say that Christ might make the world perfect without our aid. Of course He *could*. He could leave you and you and you and me out, and do His divine task alone. But God *chooses* to take you with Him in His search for other souls. He *chooses* not to leave you out of His work. Why? Because He is training you to join Jesus in the divine family; and you grow while blessing others, as much as they grow. A teacher learns while teaching. We are saved by saving.

21

Fourth Corollary: His Will Directs My Will

He is in me wherever His will directs my will to *act* or *speak* or *think*. He is in my *mind* when I have Him in mind, that is to say, when I am thinking about Him. He is in my tongue when I am talking about Him or to Him. He is in my eyes when I am seeking to help someone in need. He is in my fingers if I am writing about Him or for Him or serving a need. He is in my feet if they are carrying me to do His will. So that song, "Take My Life" is perfect:

> Take my life, and let it be
> Consecrated, Lord, to Thee;
> Take my hands, and let them move
> At the impulse of Thy love.
>
> Take my feet, and let them be
> Swift and beautiful for Thee;
> Take my voice, and let me sing
> Always, only, for my King.
>
> Take my will and make it Thine;
> It shall be no longer mine;
> Take my heart, it is Thine own!
> It shall be Thy royal throne.

Let us try to form a mental picture of Christ inhabiting our bodies. We ourselves are spirits inhabiting our own bodies. Where *life* courses through our veins, that is *our* spirit. So when *He* comes in, His Spirit inhabits our bodies along with our own spirit. Spirit, my spirit intermingled with His, can ride through the nerves like electricity, through the arteries and veins like blood corpuscles.

Spirit is as free as thought, and far swifter than light. Light traveling 186,300 miles a second takes eight minutes to reach here from the sun. But my thoughts can go to the end of the universe in the flash of a second. We may take a trip with our imagination to the other side of the moon, and back in an instant. Or to the beginning of time—we can think ourselves there in a flash. Spirit and thought are subject neither to space nor to time. With our thoughts we can bridge the abyss of the past or of the future, or the infinitely great space, or the infinitesimally small interior of an atom, before the watch can tick a second. Thoughts are spirit and love is spirit, and life is spirit, and Christ is spirit.

Fifth Corollary: Our Single Job Is To Listen and Say "Yes"

There is nothing we need to do but keep repeating over and over and over and over . . . "This house is all yours, Lord. What next?" That seems to make us perfect conductors, like pure copper wire. That willingness of surrender to Him opens the channel, clears the wire, and He does His perfect will. So if you want to be one of us who have made the great surrender, here is what to say: "Lord Jesus Christ, come into my heart, into every part of my mind and body. Here is Thy mouth, here is Thy brain, here are Thine eyes, here is Thy heart, here are Thy nerves, here are Thy muscles and veins and arteries. This is all Thy house, this is henceforth all Thy business. I am Thy servant, Thy junior partner."

Say that aloud—*mean* it—and the rest is His part. You do not know for *sure* whether this is true, unless you try it. In fact you are not really scientific unless you subject it to the test. But there cannot be even one reservation; it is all or nothing. Millions have tried to make a partial test and it did not work. Millions of us who went the whole way shout with triumphant joy as we tell you it is wonderful.

23

If this indwelling of Christ is the most important fact of any life, we want more than assurance that it is possible. We want to know how to make it a permanent fact in our own lives. How can we realize His presence, how can we remember that He rules and shares? Millions of people before us have asked this question, and have experimented until they achieved partial or perhaps complete success.

If Christ and the Father and the Holy Spirit fill *all* space, they fill every corner of our brain, every corner of our hearts, every vein and nerve and bone, every hand and foot and eye and ear and mouth. How can we be reminded of this? One may visualize with his imagination the word "Christ" blazing on the inside of his eyelids when he closes his eyes. One may visualize small signs all over his brain, bearing the word, "Christ, Christ, Christ. . . ." One may see these little signs in his own heart, in his veins and arteries, in his nerves to the ends of his fingers and toes—millions of these signs all through his body. To realize that Christ fills the body and mind of our friends we may visualize those tiny sign posts all through their bodies when we look at them.

This may seem inconsequential, but actually trying it seems to us to make a difference in the way others treat us, and we are *sure* it makes a difference in the way *we treat them* and think about them. We are *sure* too that the practice of this habit keeps us eagerly obeying what we believe God wishes of us.

This is not something to play with at odd moments, but to work at assiduously, day after day, until it becomes such a fixed habit that it requires little or no effort to recall it, *every time we close our eyelids,* every time we think.

Sixth Corollary: Bliss Is Ours

We who have tried this find that when our surrender is perfect, without holding a single corner of ourselves away from Him, He enters and fills us with an astonishing sweetness. He calls us by names as intimate as "beloved," and the intimacy we have with Him, when the surrender is perfect, is the sweetest experience any human being ever enjoys. Jesus compared it to a wedding.

To the surrendered soul He is a lover so beautiful that all the other loves are nothing. Paul was speaking from his heart when he said: "I count everything in the world as loss for the greatest gain of all—the gain of having Christ Jesus my Lord. For his sake I have lost everything and count it as waste to be thrown away so that I may have Christ and be with him" (Philippians 3:7, 8).

The Song of Songs has often been used as the most beautiful symbol of the marriage of the soul to Christ. It describes the bliss of two lovers who are totally abandoned to one another. The total abandonment of the soul to Christ often results in a mystical ecstasy so profound that the soul exhausts the language of love trying to reveal it.

> The love of Jesus, what it is
> None but his loved ones know.

Seventh Corollary: Christ Leaves Us If We Disobey

But—the moment our will revolts against Christ's will, the sweetness turns to an ugly feeling of guilt and loneliness. He steps out and then heaven is gone. The joy turns to pain. It is similar to the wall which falls between lovers when they quarrel and find their bliss suddenly turned to grief and disgust.

25

One of the most common causes of this revolt of our will is our supposed "education." The educated person may say that this is "oversimplification" or "childish." If it offends you because of its simplicity, you are lost. "I thank thee, Father, Lord of heaven and earth," said Jesus, "that thou hast hidden this from the wise and understanding and revealed it unto babes." It is easy for an infant, but impossible for those who cannot get their own critical self-importance out of the way. If a man says he will not surrender until his intellectual problems are solved, he is lost. For surrender is necessary—before we can know.

Jesus said: "He that wills to do his will shall know. . . ." Only experience can prove to the soul how surrender is the immediate doorway to the divine inflowing. The moment we surrender, we are deluged with God. And that is the proof. Christ does keep knocking until we open the door, but He does not come in until we say with total sincerity: "I surrender all: all to Thee, my blessed Saviour, I surrender all."

> How silently, how silently
> The wondrous gift is giv'n!
> So God imparts to human hearts
> The blessings of His heaven.
> No ear may hear His coming,
> But in this world of sin,
> Where meek souls will receive Him, still
> The dear Christ enters in.

Eighth Corollary: All in Whom He Dwells Are His Church

Every soul in whom Christ has found a glad welcome becomes part of His Church. So Paul says: "The whole body of the church is joined to him and each part is joined to every other. You are a body of Christ; the church is the whole body of Christ." A church building is not a "church," it is only where a church meets. The Christ-filled people are the church.

When Jesus of Nazareth began to make the world over into the Kingdom of God, He started something so vast that the one human body of Jesus was not enough. His one body could walk only in Palestine. At Pentecost the Spirit of Christ entered 120 persons, and then Christ had 120 bodies. But 120 were not enough. Outside Damascus, Christ entered Saul of Tarsus. Then He entered hundreds, then thousands. Even that many were not enough for the vast world task before Him. Christ has been reincarnated in a billion bodies. But that was not enough! He is *not* finished until His love captures *every* heart and fills *every* body. The whole human race must become His body, and the sons of man together become the dwelling place of the Son of man. This is what Paul saw when he told the Church in Ephesus: "The *church* is Christ's body and we its members are parts of the whole body of Christ."

Since there are millions born every day, His task will go on and on and on as long as women give birth. He must save the world all over again, each generation. He must stand and knock at the door of every person in the human race and wait for His chance to enter and beget a new son of God. If this makes you literally dizzy, it does me too. For it is *we* who stand at the door of other hearts and knock with Him. *Every* soul seeking to win another to Christ is really Christ Himself reaching out from within one body and pleading to enter another. His method of saving the world is "Each One Teach One and Reach One for Jesus."

If we include all Christians, the following lines— changing "my" to "our"—are true:

> He has no hands but our hands,
> No feet but our feet,
> No eyes but our eyes,
> No voice but our voice.

One may use the analogy of the living cells in the human body. Each cell is alive as a part of your body. So Paul says: "Once it was all dark within you, but now the Lord is in you and you are full of light." "It is God who shines in our hearts where it was dark."

Sociology teaches that an "organism" need not be all in one place and fastened together physically. A hive of bees is an organism. A home is an organism; so is a school, so is a political party. There are two small creatures which, when they come to a filter, simply set all their cells loose and each cell passes through a different hole in the filter. On the other side of the filter the cells reunite. All of us together are an "organism" called the church. All of us are the body of Christ, whether we are in one place or far apart.

Christ is also in every other person who surrenders to His will. So you can look into the eyes of those who love Christ and see Him there; others can look into your eyes and see Christ there. The love that binds us is more than human.

> Love divine, all loves excelling,
> Joy of heaven, to earth come down;
> *Fix in us Thy humble dwelling,*
> All Thy faithful mercies crown;
>
> Jesus, Thou art all compassion,
> Pure, unbounded love Thou art;
> Visit us with Thy salvation,
> *Enter every trembling heart.*

He is not only in saints, but also in all who are "weary and heavy laden." He said in that astonishing twenty-fifth chapter of Matthew: "I was hungry, thirsty, naked, sick, in prison and a stranger . . . and ye ministered unto me. . . . Inasmuch as you did it unto one of the least of these . . . you did it unto me." He is in every beggar, every invalid, every prisoner, calling us to love.

Christians ought not to fight one another. A cancer is a group of cells in a body which revolt and destroy the rest of the body. "We who are in Christ are one body; there is only one Holy Spirit; we ought to be one. He is in us all; He works through us all."

Ninth Corollary: Christ in Us Is Full of Miracles

If Christ is continuing to do the work which He began to do when He walked as Jesus of Nazareth in Palestine, we may expect any surprise. We never know what wonderful thing may happen next. Paul said: "When God's power is working in us, he can do more than we dare to ask or even think." "His power in us who believe, is great beyond all measure. It is the same mighty power that worked in Christ. By that power God raised him from the dead."

So! When He comes in and starts business, we are likely to be surprised by any kind of miracle! Diseases may vanish with our prayers. Mountains may be moved. The world may applaud. One has every reason to stand on tiptoe with expectancy. For God loves surprises, and He can do anything. The motto is right which says: "Expect great things from God. Attempt great things for God."

29

Tenth Corollary: We Must Avoid the Peril of Spiritual Pride

He would do even greater things if we could do them without getting "puffed up." Many a man has swollen with conceit and pride when these miracles came. So God finds a way to keep us humble. Paul tells the Corinthian Church about the visions he had, how he "was caught up to the third heaven, and then in paradise heard things which cannot be told, things which no man dare speak." Then in that paragraph Paul says: "To keep me from being too full of joy about the wonders which Christ revealed in me, he has let me suffer. . . . Three times I asked the Lord to save me from this trouble. But God said to me: 'My grace is enough for you. When you are weak then my power is made perfect.'" "For the sake of Christ I am content to be weak, to be called evil names, to suffer, to be ill-treated, to face disasters. For when I am weak, then I find I am strong."

The experience of the inrushing of the Christ Spirit brings a subtle temptation. It is so wonderful that the happy soul is in danger of imagining that he *alone* is so much favored by God. That illusion can lead to an extreme egotism and exclusiveness. It can be spiritual snobbery. It is the chief cause of the new sects which deny the validity of all other religions but their own. The fallacy is, "I am right, so everybody who differs from me is wrong." Emerson startled us by saying, "The exclusive in religion excludes only himself."

Selfishness often enters spiritual circles under a new disguise; the self tries to be superior to others. It is the same selfishness that will take all the land or all the wealth, leaving nothing for others. Sanctimonious selfishness will try to monopolize the world of the spirit. This religious pride proves that we had not surrendered all, for we had not thrown out our selfish ambition to be ahead of others. Competition has no place in the Kingdom.

Any man who thinks he has a corner on God is very ignorant—for this inflowing of divine glory is happening all over the world, all day, every day. It may come in a million ways. Since Christ loves to be in the humblest and most unnoticed little persons, especially in unattractive people, you and I ought to look deep into gentle eyes and search for Him there. The Beatitudes tell us that it comes most easily to "the poor in spirit, the meek, those who mourn."

When trouble or persecution come, we may ask whether God may be using these means to preserve our humility.

Eleventh Corollary: Christ in Us May Be Crucified Again

If Christ lives in you and me, He still goes to the cross in us as He did in the early martyrs. Paul does not say much about the miracles which Christ worked through him, but Paul says a great deal about *suffering with Christ:* "I am willing to share his suffering and to die as he died. For his sake I have lost everything. I am happy to suffer for your sakes. In my flesh I am completing Christ's suffering for his church. . . . I am in prison for what I preach. We Christians must expect to suffer. Remember my prison chains. Silas and I have been terribly beaten and you know how we suffered. Perhaps my life blood may soon be poured out as a sacrifice to God for your faith. If so I shall be glad to go. I am crucified with Christ."

The noblest power Christ gave Paul and the early Christians was the power to hang with Him on a cross with divine courage. Paul says: "Oh, how I suffered in

Macedonia! When I reached there my poor body had no peace. I met with trouble on every side. . . . But God comes to the help of those whose hearts are heavy. I have had a very large share in Christ's sufferings. . . . Be patient when you suffer, as I am patient. Then I shall be comforted in my sorrow. . . . I know that you have suffered just as I have. . . . I have had to go through sufferings, difficulties, terrible troubles, beatings, prisons, angry crowds, hard labor, nights without sleep, hunger."

This kind of power—power to endure the cross—is what we may expect when we let Christ in. It may not be a suffering of our own choosing. If it were, it might be more bearable. But it is most likely to be the cross we do not want to bear.

Yet we do not suffer alone. When He is in us and we suffer, He is sharing His sufferings with us. We never understand the cross of Christ until we hang on our cross with Him. Here is a strange poem by Elizabeth Cheney:

> Whenever there is silence around me
> By day or by night—
> I am startled by a cry.
> It came down from the cross—
> The first time I heard it.
> I went out and searched—
> And found a man in the throes of crucifixion,
> And I said, "I will take you down,"
> And I tried to take the nails out of his feet.
> But he said, "Let them be
> For I cannot be taken down
> Until every man, every woman, and every child
> Come together to take me down."

How could that be true? Jesus of Nazareth was taken down from the cross by Joseph of Arimathea and buried.

Jesus of Nazareth is no longer on a cross. But if He is reincarnated in us, then He is crucified anew when we are crucified. Paul said, "I am crucified with Christ." On Calvary there were three who suffered together, Jesus and two criminals. When we take up our cross, there are two of us who suffer together. Christ and I suffer together for the sins of the world, including my own. Multitudes of people have endured suffering with singing souls because they discovered that He endures every pain with us. The strangest paradox in Christianity is that it is a mingling of infinite agony and infinite bliss.

Most of us for most of our lives have run away from the agony which Paul and many in the early church endured all their lives. We have learned how to pick the rose without the thorns. But at times we ask ourselves: "Is this what Christ meant when He said, 'Unless you take up your cross and follow me, you cannot be my disciple'?"

We do not sing now what they sang in the days they suffered:

> Must I be carried to the skies
>   On flowery beds of ease,
> While others fought to win the prize
>   And sailed through bloody seas?

Nobody should go out just to seek suffering as the flagellants do, when they flog themselves until they bleed. But if we go out *to save the lost*, we shall meet enemies and crosses on the way, and then we must choose between saving ourselves and others. The Old Testament tells of priests who took good care of themselves while their sheep were wandering and lost. But Jesus did not take care of Himself. While He suffered on the cross, His enemies told the deepest truth ever told about Him, when they wagged their fingers at His agony and with raucous laughter said: "Ha, ha, ha, He saved *others,* but He cannot save *Himself.*"

That was the ultimate compliment! He could not do both, so He chose not to save *Himself!* But those men at the foot of the cross were so blinded with taking good care of themselves that they did not know they were gazing upon the supreme nobility. Jesus could have saved Himself just by stopping at Jericho, or halfway up the mountain road to Jerusalem, or by staying in Bethany, but "he set his face to go to Jerusalem"—and that cross. Our daily temptation is to avoid the cross, and save ourselves by sacrificing others. Most people save themselves just by saying "No" to the call to climb the hill to Calvary. Men have often saved themselves, letting the rest perish. But Paul went all the way, saying: "Christ took me to the cross with him, and I died with him. It is no longer I that live, Christ is living in me." "We shall rise with him if we suffer with him."

Yet to stress pain too much would be wrong. For when He shares our pain He turns it into bliss. The martyrs could be burned singing at the stake. They could be flung to the lions, praising God. They felt no pain.

Twelfth Corollary: We Can Forget Self If Christ Is Inside

Jesus said in the Sermon on the Mount: "Do not be anxious." We cannot help being anxious if He is not in us. But if He is inside we can forget about ourselves and be anxious only for others, not about what we shall wear or eat or drink. There are three reasons why we can forget ourselves:

First, my Senior Partner knows everything. I do not need to know much, because He knows what I do not know and He will tell me when He is ready to tell me. He has been here since the worlds were made, and nothing has escaped Him. He knows every answer. I know very little, but *my Senior Partner and I together know everything*.

Second, He can do anything. He made it all and there is nothing He cannot change, the moment He wants to change it. I am weak, but He and I can do anything. I have no power, but in my weakness His power shines forth. He does not do everything at my bidding, but I can do anything at *His* bidding. He and I together can do anything, if He wants it.

Third, He loves me. I can trust Him a great deal better than I can trust myself. I have often been my own worst enemy, hurting myself by hate and sin and pettiness. But Christ never fails to do His best for me. He loves me more than I love myself. So with Paul I can say: "I am persuaded that neither life nor death, nor things now present nor things to come, nor heights nor depths nor anything else can separate me from the love of Christ." This is why many Christians go through life singing, in the midst of persecutions: "Oh, it is wonderful, very, very wonderful. . . ."

Inside, it is heaven. For heaven is where Jesus is. So Paul could rejoice in prison. From his prison in Rome he wrote most amazing things: "My prayers are always full of joy . . . I want you to know that my being in prison has helped the good news spread. . . . That fills me with joy. Yes, I am going right on being full of joy. . . . For me to live is Christ, and to die is gain. . . . I cannot tell which to choose, life or death. I want to go and be with Christ. That will be for me better. But I think he needs me more here in this body for your sakes. So I expect to remain and continue to help you. . . . But perhaps my life blood may soon be poured out as a sacrifice to God for your faith. If so I am glad to go, and I shall thank God with you. I want you to be glad, too, and to thank God."

The Twenty-third Psalm suddenly comes alive with new meaning if we say it remembering that Christ lives in us:

> The Lord in my heart is my shepherd. I shall not want.
> He who is in my heart maketh me to lie down in green pastures . . .
> He who is in my heart restoreth my soul.
> He leadeth me in the paths of righteousness for his name's sake . . .
> Yea, though I walk through the valley of the shadow of death,
> I will fear no evil, for thou art in me.
> Thy rod and thy staff they comfort me.
> Thou preparest a table before me in the presence of mine enemies;
> Thou anointest my head with oil;
> My cup runneth over.
> Surely goodness and mercy shall follow me all the days of my life;
> And I will dwell in the house of the Lord for ever.

When Christ lives in me, life is exciting. For He is powerful beyond words or limits—He can do anything, change anything, stop anything. Not, we must remember, at *our* bidding, but when *He* desires. We are in partnership with a miracle worker! He loves variety and beauty—look at the flowers! and listen to great music!

Thirteenth Corollary: We Can Talk to One Another Inside

If Christ is inside, then He and I can talk to one another inside. He may use these lips, for they are His. I may use them to talk or ask Him questions, for they are also my lips. So the same pair of lips are for Him to talk to me, and for me to talk to Him.

Or when there are people around or when we do not feel like talking aloud, we may talk in whispers down in our breast to one another. Walter Rauschenbusch said this exquisitely in his poem "The Postern Gate":

> In the castle of my soul
> Is a little postern gate,
> Whereat, when I enter,
> I am in the presence of God.
> In a moment, in the turning of a thought,
> I am where God is.
> This is a fact.
>
> *   *   *
>
> When I am with God
> I look deep down and high up,
> And all is changed.
>
> *   *   *
>
> With God is great silence.
> But that silence is a melody
> Sweet as the contentment of love,
> Thrilling as a touch of flame.
>
> *   *   *
>
> When I enter into God,
> All life has a meaning.
>
> Without asking I know;
> My desires are even now fulfilled,

My fever is gone
In the great quiet of God.

* * *

When I am in the consciousness of God,
My fellow men are not far-off and forgotten,
But close and strangely dear.
Those whom I love
Have a mystic value.
They shine, as if a light were glowing within them.
Even those who frown on me
And love me not
Seem part of the great scheme of Good.

* * *

When I am in him, I am in the Kingdom of God
And in the Fatherland of my Soul.

How can one be sure that the conviction he feels, or
this inner "voice," is from Christ and not from the devil?
That is a very serious question and often it is a difficult
question. One dare not trust his conscience . . . not unless it is an educated conscience. Conscience told our pious
ancestors to burn witches and heretics. The only way to
educate the conscience is to *memorize the life and teach-
ings of Jesus.* We ought to accompany Him across the
Gospel pages until His response to every question will at
once flash into the memory. It is important to have a
regular hour each day when we will be uninterrupted by
telephone or television or children. Our reading should be
leisurely and delightful. We can whisper to Him about
every verse. When we know His life and words perfectly,
we shall have a perfect standard by which to test whether
our ideas are from Him or from some other source.

When He enters our souls and a new creature is born,
He puts in us a keen appetite to know all about Him. We

shall thrill to read and reread His life until we know it by heart. Then we will not be guided so much by advice from others as we will by directions from *Him*.

Fourteenth Corollary: A Little Constant Pressure of the Will Is Necessary

One who tries to live this experience and not just talk about it, finds that it demands a little pressure of the will a good part of the time. It is easy to forget, hard not to forget. So many of us, while in this learning period, surround ourselves with memory aids—pictures of Jesus, books that remind us, music that reminds us, mottoes that remind us—so that whatever direction we look we are reminded of Christ. It becomes a habit.

At times one experiences rebellion of the will. We sometimes want to take a vacation from religion altogether. Our taste may call for a mystery or a football game. If the thing we crave is not wrong, we can take Jesus with us, and enjoy the story or the game all the more. There is nothing in the universe outside His interest.

The Reverend A. B. Simpson, founder of the Christian and Missionary Alliance, has had wonderful experiences of the indwelling Christ. Let him tell it himself:

He said to me—oh so tenderly—"My child, just take Me and let Me be in you, Myself." I placed my eyes on the Christ in me, and found Him larger than the moment's need, the Christ that had all I should ever need. When I thus saw Him it was all right, and right forever.

He said to me: "My child, you must come to Me for the next breath, because I love you so dearly I want you to come all the time. If I gave you a great supply you would do without Me, and would not come to Me so often; now you have to come to Me every second, and lie on My breast every moment."

I had to learn to take from Him my spiritual life every second; to breathe Him in and to breathe myself out. You say, "Is that not a terrible bondage to be always on that strain?" On the strain with one you love, with your dearest Friend? No, it comes as naturally as a fountain, without effort—for true life with Him is always easy and overflowing.

Now I have Him; not only what I have room for, but that which I do not yet have room for, but I shall be full whenever I have room, in the eternity that lies ahead of me. I am like a little bottle in the sea, as full as it can hold. As the bottle is in the sea, so I am in Christ and Christ is in me; and there is a whole oceanful beyond. . . .

God seemed to speak to me so sweetly: "Never mind, my child, if you have nothing, for I have the power, and the love and the faith, and the blessing you need. I am all you need within, and all you need without forever."

Simpson and his courageous missionaries over the world have discovered that the secret of radiant living is, "Christ in and around me like the bottle in the sea." The gallant missionaries of all communions scattered in remote corners are the best incarnations of Jesus I have ever seen.

Fifteenth Corollary: Christ Returns in Every Follower

The "Second Coming of Christ" did take place at Pentecost and He has been coming ever since. For two thousand years—since that first Pentecost when His Spirit entered 120 of His followers—His Spirit has entered and dwelt inside countless millions of His humble followers. He has been here every moment of every year—in them! He is more than a disembodied Spirit—He is embodied right now in millions upon millions all over this world. He *has* come again. He *will* come again. As Rabindranath Tagore says, "He comes, He comes, He ever comes." Mil-

lions in every land welcomed Him when He knocked—
they surrendered their wills to His, He took possession,
He began to reach out and look out and walk out and love
out through them. I have seen a million incarnations of
Christ with my own eyes.

And now, Christ, you inside me are turning round and
round and round in all directions, looking, looking, looking, for some door on which to knock, where a heart will
open, a spirit will receive your Spirit, and a *new birth*
will begin which is both human and divine.

Is it true? Yes, for us who say "yes"; for us who *will*
it to be so. For the others it is not yet true. "The world
will not see me, but you will see me. . . . Because I live,
you will live."

> Where meek souls will receive Him, still
> The dear Christ enters in.

This is indeed the deepest truth in the Christian religion,
and it is the climactic event of creation!

Theologians have called it "the divine encounter," but
it is more, more, more; it is the divine penetration, the
divine rebirth, it *is* creation, for behold . . . *a new creature*.

Dear friends who understand what I mean, we must
have endless patience with those who cannot see this. We
must wait in patience. The direction in which they go
may end in some shipwreck—they then will reach for a
hand to rescue them, and He will be there waiting. Every
disaster can be God's doorway to heaven.

Jesus said, "I thank thee, Father, Lord of heaven and
earth, that thou hast hidden this from the wise and understanding and revealed it unto babes."

41

GAME WITH MINUTES

Game With Minutes

CHRIST IS THE ONLY HOPE OF THE WORLD

"Disillusioned by all our other efforts, we now see that the only hope left for the human race is to become like Christ." That is the statement of a famous scientist, and is being repeated among ever more educators, statesmen, and philosophers. Yet Christ has not saved the world from its present terrifying dilemma. The reason is obvious: Few people are getting enough of Christ to save either themselves or the world. Take the United States, for example. Only about half of the population belongs to a Christian church. Less than half of this number attend services regularly. Good sermons, many of them excellent, too infrequently present Christ.

A few minutes a week given to thinking about Christ by one-fourth of the people is not saving our country or our world; for selfishness, greed, and hate are getting a thousand times that much thought. What a nation thinks about, that it is. We shall not become like Christ until we give Him more time. A teachers' college requires students to attend classes for twenty-five hours a week for three years. Could it prepare competent teachers or a law school prepare competent lawyers if they studied only ten minutes a week? Neither can Christ, and He never pretended that He could. To His disciples He said: "Come with me, walk with me, talk and listen to me, work and

44

rest with me, eat and sleep with me, twenty-four hours a day for three years." That was their college course—"He chose them," the Bible says, "that they might be with him," 168 hours a week!

All who have tried that kind of abiding for a month know the power of it—it is like being born again from center to circumference. It absolutely changes every person who does it. And it will change the world that does it.

How can a man or woman take this course with Christ today? The answer is so simple a child can understand it. Indeed, unless we "turn and become like children" we shall not succeed.

This is how:

1. We have a study hour. We read and reread the life of Jesus recorded in the Gospels, thoughtfully and prayerfully at least an hour a day. We find new translations and fresh ways of reading so it will never be dull, but always stimulating and inspiring. We walk with Jesus through Galilee by walking with Him through the pages of His earthly history.

2. We make Him our companion. We try to call Him to mind at least one second of each minute. We do not need to forget other things nor stop our work, but we invite Him to share everything we do or say or think. Hundreds of us have experimented until we have found ways to let Him share every minute of our waking hours. In fact, it is no harder to learn this new habit than to learn the touch system in typing, and in time one can win a high percentage of his minutes with as little effort as an expert uses to write a letter.

While this takes all our time, yet it does not take it from any other good enterprise. We take Christ into that enterprise and make it more resultful. It also keeps a man's religion steady. If the temperature of a sick man rises and falls daily the doctor regards him as seriously ill. This is the case with religion. Not spiritual chills and fevers, but an abiding faith which gently presses the will toward Christ all day, is a sign of a healthy religion.

Practicing the presence of God is not on trial. It has already been proven by countless thousands of people. Indeed, the spiritual giants of all ages have known it. Christians who do it today become more fervent and beautiful and are tireless witnesses. Men and women who had been slaves of vices have been set free. Catholics and Protestants agree that practicing the presence of God is at the heart of their faith. Conservatives and liberals agree that here is a reality they need. Letters from all parts of the world testify that in this game multitudes are turning defeat into victory and despair into joy.

The results of this program begin to show clearly in a month. They grow rich after six months, and glorious after ten years.

Someone may be saying, "What is new about this? It is very orthodox and very ancient." It is, indeed, the secret of the great saints of all ages.

"Pray without ceasing," said Paul, "in everything make your wants known unto God." "As many as are *led* by the Spirit of God, these are the sons of God."

HOW WE WIN THE GAME WITH MINUTES

No one is wholly satisfied with himself. Our lives are made up of lights and shadows, of some good days and many unsatisfactory days. Every real Christian knows that the good days and hours come when we are close to Christ, and that the poor days come whenever we push Him out of our thoughts. Clearly, then, the way to a more consistent high level is to take Him into everything we do or say or think.

Good resolutions are not enough. Experience has told

us that we need to discipline our lives to an ordered regime. The "Game with Minutes" is a rather lighthearted name for such a regime in the realm of the spirit. Many of us have found it to be enormously helpful. It is a new game for something as old as Enoch, who "walked with God." It is a way of living which nearly everybody knows and nearly everybody has ignored.

We call this a "game" because it is delightful fun and an exhilarating spiritual exercise; but it is far more than a game. Perhaps a better name for it would be "an exploratory expedition," because it opens out into what seems at first to be a beautiful garden; then the garden widens into a country; and at last we realize that we are exploring a new world. This may sound like poetry, but it is not overstating what experience has shown us. Some people have compared it to getting out of a dark prison and beginning to *live*. We still see the same world, yet it is not the same for it has a new glorious color and a far richer meaning. Thank God, this adventure is free for everybody, rich or poor, wise or ignorant, famous or unknown, with a good past or a bad—"Whosoever will, may come." The greatest thing in the world is for everyone!

You will find this just as easy and just as hard as forming any other habit. You have hitherto thought of God for only a few seconds or minutes a week, and He was out of your mind the rest of the time. Students will at once recognize this as a fresh approach to Brother Lawrence's "Practicing the Presence of God." You are attempting, like Brother Lawrence, to have God in mind each minute you are awake. Such drastic change in habit requires a real effort at the beginning.

Many of us find it very useful to have pictures of Christ where our eyes will fall on them every time we look around. A very happy hobby is to collect the most

47

friendly pictures of Christ, pocket size, so that we can erect our own shrine in a few seconds.

HOW TO BEGIN

Select a favorable hour; try how many minutes of the hour you can remember God at least *once* each minute; that is to say, bring God to mind at least one second out of every sixty. It is not necessary to remember God *every second,* for the mind runs along like a rapid stream from one idea to another.

Your score will be low at first, but keep trying, for it constantly becomes easier, and after a while is almost automatic. It follows the well-known laws of habit forming. If you try to write shorthand you are at first very awkward. This is true when you are learning to play a piano, or to ride a bicycle, or to use any new muscles. When you try this "Game with Minutes" you discover that spiritually you are still a very weak infant. A babe in the crib seizes upon everything at hand to pull himself to his feet, wabbles for a few seconds and falls exhausted. Then he tries again, each time standing a little longer than before. We are like that babe when we begin to try to keep God in mind. We need something to which we can cling. Our minds wabble and fall, then rise for a new effort. Each time we try we shall do better until at last we may be able to remember God as high as 90 per cent of the whole day.

HOW TO TRY THE EXPERIMENT IN CHURCH

You have a good chance of starting well if you begin in church—provided the sermon is about God. When our congregation first tried it, we distributed slips of paper which read:

At the opening of the service the pastor made this announcement: "Everyone will be asked to fill this score card at the end of one hour. In order to succeed, you may use any help within reach. You may look at the cross, or you may leaf through your hymnbook or Bible, looking for the verses that remind you of God."

The sermon that Sunday explained how to play the game. At the end of the hour, the score cards were collected. The congregation reported scores ranging from five to sixty minutes. The average was forty-four minutes, which meant 73 per cent of the hour. For beginners this was excellent. Such an experiment, by the way, will encourage the congregation to listen better than usual, and will remind the preacher to keep his sermon close to God.

If you score 75 per cent in church, you can probably make a rather good score for the rest of the day. It is a question of being master of every new situation.

Never use a score card more than an hour, and not that long if it tires you. This is a new delight you are learning, and it must not be turned into a task.

WHILE GOING HOME FROM CHURCH

Can you win your Game with Minutes while passing people on the street? Yes! Experiments have revealed a sure way to succeed: offer a swift prayer for the people at whom you glance. It is easy to think an instantaneous prayer while looking people straight in the eye, and the way people smile back at you shows that they like it! This practice gives a surprising exhilaration, as you may prove for yourself. A half-hour spent walking and praying for all one meets, instead of tiring one, gives him a sense of ever heightening energy like a battery being charged. It is a tonic, a good way to overcome a tired feeling.

Some of us walk on the right side of the pavement, leaving room for our unseen Friend, whom we visualize walking by our side, and we engage in silent conversations with Him about the people we meet. For example, we may say: "Dear Companion, what can we do together for this man whom we are passing?" Then we whisper what we believe Christ would answer.

WHERE TO LOOK FOR CHRIST

We have a right to use any aid that proves useful. One such aid is to think of Christ as in a definite location. To be sure, He is a Spirit, everywhere at once—and therefore anywhere we realize Him to be. Many of us win our game nearly all of some days by realizing His unseen presence sitting in a chair or walking beside us. Some of us have gazed at our favorite picture of Him until it floats before our memories whenever we glance at His unseen presence, and we almost see Him. Indeed, many of us do see Him in our dreams. Others, like St. Paul, like to feel Him within the breast; many, like St. Patrick, feel Him all around us, above, below, before, behind, as though we walked in His kindly halo. We may have our secret ways of helping us to realize that He is very near and very dear.

ON A TRAIN OR IN A CROWD

We whisper "God" or "Jesus" or "Christ" constantly as we glance at every person near us. We try to see *double,* as Christ does—we see the person as he is and the person Christ longs to make of him. Remarkable things happen, until those in tune look around as though you spoke—especially children. The atmosphere of a room changes when a few people keep whispering to Him about all the rest. Perhaps there is no finer ministry than just to be in meetings or crowds, whispering "Jesus," and then helping people whenever you see an opportunity. When Dr. Allan Chalmers answers the telephone, he whispers: "A child of God will now speak to me." We can do that when anyone speaks to us.

If everyone in America would do the things just described above, we should have a "heaven below." This is not pious poetry. We have *seen* what happens. Try it during all this week, until a strange power develops within you. As messages from England are broadcast in Long Island for all America, so we can become spiritual broadcasters for Christ. Every cell in our brain is an electric battery which He can use to intensify what He longs to say to people who are spiritually too deaf to hear Him without our help.

WHILE IN CONVERSATION

Suppose when you reach home you find a group of friends engaged in ordinary conversation. Can you remember God at least once every minute? This is hard, but we have found that we can be successful if we employ

51

some reminders. Here are aids which have proven useful:

1. Have a *picture* of Christ in front of you where you can glance at it frequently.

2. Have an *empty chair* beside you and imagine that your Unseen Master is sitting in it; if possible reach your hand and touch that chair, as though holding His hand. He is there, for He said: "Lo, I am with you always."

3. Keep humming to yourself a favorite *prayer hymn*— for example, "Have Thine Own Way, Lord, Have Thine Own Way."

4. Silently *pray* for each person in the circle.

5. Keep *whispering* inside: "Lord, put Thy thoughts in my mind. Tell me what to say."

6. Best of all, tell your companions about the "Game with Minutes." If they are interested, you will have no more trouble. *You cannot keep God unless you give Him to others.*

WHEN AT THE TABLE

All the previous suggestions are useful at mealtime. If possible, have an empty chair for your Invisible Guest, who said, "Wherever two or three are gathered together, I am in the midst." Another useful aid is to recall what the Quakers believe about every meal. Jesus told us: "Eat this in remembrance of me." The Friends think that He meant, not only consecrated bread, but all food, so that every mouthful is His "body broken for you."

You might read and discuss this book. It helps immediately if others at the table agree to try to win this mealtime together.

WHILE READING A BOOK

When we are reading a newspaper or magazine or book, we read it to Him! We often glance at the empty chair where we visualize Him, or at His picture, and continue a running conversation with Him inwardly about the pages we are reading. Kagawa says scientific books are letters from God telling how He runs His universe.

Have you ever opened a letter and read it *with* Jesus, realizing that He smiles with us at the fun, rejoices with us in the successes, and weeps with us at life's tragedies? If not, you have missed one of life's sweetest experiences.

WHEN THINKING

If you lean back and think about some problem deeply, how can you remember God? You can do it by forming a new habit. All thought employs silent words and is really conversation with your inner self. Instead of talking to yourself, you will now form the habit of talking to Christ. Many of us who have tried this have found that we think so much better that we never want to try to think without Him again. We are helped if we imagine Him sitting in a chair beside us, talking with us. We say with our tongues what we think Christ might say in reply to our questions. Thus we *consult* Christ about everything.

No practice we have ever found has held our thinking so uniformly high and wholesome as this making all thought a *conversation with God*. When evil thoughts of any kind come, we say, "Lord, these thoughts are not fit to discuss with Thee. Think Thy thoughts in my mind." The result is an instantaneous purification.

Turn every thought into conversation with God.

WHEN WALKING ALONE

If you are strolling out-of-doors alone, you can recall God at least once every minute with no effort, if you remember that "beauty is the voice of God." Every flower and tree, river and lake, mountain and sunset, is God speaking. "This is my Father's world, and to my listening ears all nature sings. . . ." So as you look at each lovely thing, you may keep asking: "Dear Father, what are you telling me through this, and this, and this?"

If you have wandered to a place where you can talk aloud without being overheard, you may speak to the Invisible Companion inside you or beside you. Ask Him what is most on His heart and then answer back aloud with your voice what you believe God would reply to you.

Of course we are not always sure whether we have guessed God's answer right, but it is surprising how much of the time we are very certain. It really is not necessary to be sure that our answer is right, for the answer is not the great thing—He is! God is infinitely more important than His advice or His gifts; indeed, *He, Himself, is the great gift*. The youth in love does not so much prize what his sweetheart may say or may give him, as the fact that she is *his* and that she is *here*. The most precious privilege in talking with God is this intimacy which we can have with Him. We may have a glorious succession of heavenly minutes. How foolish people are to lose life's most poignant joy, seeing it may be had while taking a walk alone!

But the most wonderful discovery of all is, to use the words of St. Paul, "Christ liveth in me." He dwells in us, walks in our minds, reaches out through our hands, speaks with our voices, *if* we obey His every whisper.

BE MY LAST THOUGHT

We make sure that there is a picture of Christ, or a Bible, or a cross or some other object where it will greet our closing eyes as we fall asleep. We continue to whisper any words of endearment our hearts suggest. If all day long we have been walking with Him, we shall find Him the dear Companion of our dreams. Sometimes, after such a day, we have fallen asleep with our pillows wet from tears of joy, feeling His tender touch on our foreheads. Usually we feel no deep emotion, but always we have a "peace that passeth all understanding." This is the end of a perfect day.

MONDAY MORNING

If on Sunday we have rated over 50 per cent in our Game with Minutes, we shall be eager to try the experiment during a busy Monday. As we open our eyes and see a picture of Christ on the wall, we may ask: "Now, Master, shall we get up?" Some of us whisper to Him our every thought about washing and dressing in the morning, about brushing our shoes and choosing our clothes. Christ is interested in every trifle, because He loves us more intimately than a mother loves her babe, or a lover his sweetheart, and is happy only when we share every question with Him.

MEN AT WORK

Countless thousands of men keep God in mind while engaged in all types of work, mental or manual, and find that they are happier and get better results. Those who endure the most intolerable ordeals gain new strength when they realize that their Unseen Comrade is by their side. To be sure, no man whose business is harmful or whose methods are dishonest can expect God's partnership. But if an enterprise is useful, God eagerly shares in its real progress. The carpenter can do better work if he talks quietly to God about each task, as Jesus certainly did when He was a carpenter. Many of us have found that we can compose a letter or write a book better when we say: "God, think Thy thoughts in my mind. What

55

dost Thou desire written? Here is my hand; use it. Pour Thy wisdom through my hand." Our thoughts flow faster, and what we write is better. God loves to be a co-author!

MERCHANTS AND BANKERS

A merchant who waits on his customers and prays for them at the same time wins their affection and their business. A salesman who prays for those with whom he is dealing has far more likelihood of making a sale. A book-keeper or banker can whisper to God about every column of figures and be certain that God is even more interested in the figures than he is. The famous astronomer, Sir James Jeans, calls God the "supermathematician of the universe, making constant use of mathematical formulae that would drive Einstein mad."

IN THE HOME

Many women cultivate Christ's companionship while cooking, washing dishes, sweeping, sewing, and caring for children. Aids which they find helpful are:

1. Whispering to God about each small matter, knowing that He loves to help.

2. Humming or singing a favorite prayer hymn.

3. Showing the children how to play the Game with Minutes, and asking them to share in playing it. Children love this game and develop an inner control when they play it which renders discipline almost needless.

4. Having pictures of Christ about the house, as a constant reminder.

5. Saying to God, "Think Thy thoughts in my mind."

WHEN IN SCHOOL

An increasing army of students in school who are winning this game tell us how they do it. Here is their secret:

When in study period, say: "God, I have just forty precious minutes. Help my wavering thoughts to concentrate so that I may not waste a moment. Show me what is worth remembering in this first paragraph"—then read the lesson to God, instead of reading it to yourself.

When going to recitation, whisper: "Make my mind clear, so that I will be able to recall all I have studied. Take away fear."

When rising to recite before a group, say: "God, speak through my lips."

When taking an examination, say all during the hour, "Father, keep my mind clear, and help me to remember all that I have learned. How shall we answer this next question?" Visualize Him looking over your shoulder every minute you are writing. God will not tell you what you have never studied but He does sharpen your memory and take away your stage fright when you ask Him. Have you not discovered that when you pray about some forgotten name, it often flashes into your memory?

To be sure, this prevents us from being dishonest or cheating, for if we are not honest we cannot expect His help. But that is a good reason for playing the Game with Minutes. Character is a hundred times more valuable than knowledge or high grades.

To be popular with the other students, acquire the habit of breathing a momentary prayer for each student you meet, and while you are in conversation with him. Some instinct tells him you are interested in his welfare and he likes you for it.

PRAYING HORSESHOES

A very powerful way to pray is for a group of friends to be seated in the shape of a horseshoe. We have an altar at the open end of the horseshoe, with a cross and a pic-

57

ture of Jesus, and a globe of the world. The horseshoe opens toward the cities, countries, and people most in need of prayer.

This horseshoe of prayer reminds us of the great magnets which can lift a locomotive when the electric power is turned on. We are seeking to be used by the inpouring Holy Spirit to lift the world, and to draw all men to Christ.

It also reminds us of the radio broadcast which, when the power is on, leaps around the world. We offer ourselves as God's broadcasting station. The group may prepare a list of the most urgent world needs and of key persons.

The gentle tingle which many in these groups feel reminds us of the glow and soft purr in the tubes of a radio when the power is on.

Every Christian family at mealtime may form a prayer radio broadcast by joining hands. Young people's societies will love it. It will vitalize every Sunday-school class to spend ten minutes in broadcasting. Defunct prayer meetings will come to life when they become horseshoe magnets of prayer. Schools and colleges, public or private, will find prayer horseshoes popular with the students. Here is something that we can all do together. Worship can thus be made the most thrilling experience of our lives.

PRAY OVER THE NEWSPAPER

An excellent plan is for someone to read from the newspaper the problems and persons which are most in need of prayer that morning.

The leader may say words like these: "Lord, in this terribly critical hour we want to do everything we can. We pray Thee, use us to help the President to be hungry for Thee, to listen and hear and obey Thee. We lift our President into Thy presence." Then all may raise their clasped hands toward heaven. And so with the entire list.

After the prayer list is completed, a globe of the world may be lifted toward God while somebody prays the Lord's Prayer. Every prayer group needs a globe.

DURING PLAY HOURS

God is interested in our fun as much as we are. Many of us talk to Him during our games. Some of the famous football players long ago discovered that they played better if they prayed all during the game. Some of the famous runners pray during races. If a thing brings health and joy and friendship and a fresh mind, God is keenly interested, because He is interested in us.

While on the playground, do not ask to win, but whisper: "God get Thy will done exactly. Help us all to do our best. Give us what is far more important than defeating our opponents—make us clean sportsmen and make us good friends."

GOD AND LOVE

Sweethearts who have been wise enough to share their love with God have found it incomparably more wonderful. Since "God is Love" He is in deepest sympathy with every fond whisper and look. Husbands and wives, too, give rapturous testimony of homes transformed by praying silently when together. In some cases, where they had begun to give each other "nerves," they have found, after playing this game when they are alone together by day or by night, that their love grew strangely fresh, rich, beautiful, "Like a new honeymoon." God is the Maker of all true marriages, and He gives His highest joy to a man

59

and wife who share their love for each other with Him, who pray inwardly each for the other when they are together looking into one another's eyes. Married love becomes infinitely more wonderful when Christ is the bond every minute, and it grows sweeter as the years go by to the very last day. Imagine, too, what this does for the children!

TROUBLES

Troubles and pain come to those who practice God's presence, as they came to Jesus, but these seem trivial as compared to their new joyous experience. If we have spent our days with Him, we find that when earthquakes, fires, famines or other catastrophes threaten us, we are not terrified any more than Paul was in time of shipwreck. "Perfect love casteth out fear."

The Game with Minutes is good for people suffering from illness at home or in hospitals. Nurses remind us that the thoughts of people turn toward God when sick as at no other time. Patients who are convalescing have many idle hours when their minds reach up toward God. Playing this game produces a perfect mental state for rapid recovery.

Those who are seeking to be aware of God constantly have found that their former horror at death has vanished. We may have a new mystic intimacy with our departed loved ones, for though unseen to us, they are with Christ and since He is with us, they are with us as well.

SOME PRICES WE MUST PAY TO WIN THIS GAME

The first price is *pressure* of our wills, gentle but constant. What game is ever won without effort and concentration?

The second price is *perseverance*. A low score at the outset is not the least reason for discouragement; everybody gets a low score for a long while. Each week grows better and requires less strain.

The third price is *perfect surrender*. We lose Christ the moment our wills rebel. If we try to keep even a remote corner of life for self or evil, and refuse to let God rule us wholly, that small worm will spoil the entire fruit. We must be utterly sincere.

The fourth price is *tell others*. When anybody complains that he is losing the game, we flash this question back at him: "Are you telling your friends about it?" For you cannot keep Christ unless you give Him away.

The fifth price is *to be in a group*. We need the stimulus of a few intimate friends who exchange their experiences with us.

THE PRIZES WE WIN

It is obvious that this is unlike other games in many respects. One difference is that *we all win*. We may not win all or even half of our minutes, but we do win a richer life, which is all that really matters. There are no losers except those who quit. Let us consider some of those prizes:

1. We develop what Thomas à Kempis calls a "familiar friendship with Jesus." Our Unseen Friend becomes dearer, closer and more wonderful every day until at last we know Him as "Jesus, lover of my soul" not only in songs, but in blissful experiences. Doubts vanish, we are more sure of Him being with us than of anybody else. This warm, ardent friendship ripens rapidly until people see its glory shining in our eyes—and it keeps on growing richer and more radiant every month.

2. All we undertake is done better and more smoothly.

We have daily evidence that God helps our work, piling one proof upon another until we are sure of God, not from books or preachers, but from our own experience.

3. When we are playing this game our minds are pure as a mountain stream every moment.

4. The Bible and Christian hymns seem like different books, for they begin to sparkle with the beautiful thoughts of saints who have had glorious experiences with God. We begin to understand their bliss, for we share it with them.

5. All day long we are *contented,* whatever our lot may be, for He is with us. "When Jesus goes with me, I'll go anywhere."

6. It becomes easy to tell others about Christ because our minds are flooded with Him. "Out of the fullness of the heart the mouth speaketh."

7. Grudges, jealousies, hatred, and prejudices melt away. Little hells turn into little heavens. Communities have been transformed where this game was introduced. Love rises like a kindly sea and at last drowns all the demons of malice and selfishness. Then we see that the only hope for this insane world is to persuade people to "practice the presence of God."

8. "Genius is 90 per cent concentration." This game, like all concentration upon one objective, eventually results in flashes of new brilliant thought which astonish us, and keep us tiptoe with expectancy for the next vision which God will give us.

WHAT IS MEANT BY WINNING

You win your minute if, during that minute, you:
1. Pray.
2. Recall God.
3. Sing or hum a devotional hymn.

4. Talk or write about God.
5. Seek to relieve suffering of any kind in a prayerful spirit.
6. Work with the consciousness of God's presence.
7. Whisper to God.
8. Feel yourself encompassed by God.
9. Look at a picture or a symbol of Christ.
10. Read a Scripture verse or poem about God.
11. Give someone a helping hand for the Lord's sake.
12. Breathe a prayer for the people you meet.
13. Follow the leading of the Inner Voice.
14. Plan or work for the Kingdom of God.
15. Testify to others about God, the church, or this game.
16. Share suffering or sorrow with another.
17. Hear God and see Him in flowers, trees, water, hills, sky.

We never attempt to keep a minute-by-minute record (except perhaps occasionally for an hour), since such a record would interfere with normal life. We are practicing a new freedom, not a new bondage. We must not get so tied down to score keeping that we lose the glory of it, and its spontaneity. We fix our eyes upon Jesus, not upon a clock.

INFINITE VARIETY

The notion that religion is dull, stupid and sleepy, is abhorrent to God, for He has created infinite variety and He loves to surprise us. If you are weary of some sleepy form of devotion, probably God is as weary of it as you are. Shake out of it, and approach Him in one of the countless fresh directions. When our minds lose the edge of their zest, let us shift to another form of fellowship; turn the dial of our mental radio. Every tree, every cloud,

63

every city, every soap bubble is alive with God to those who know His language.

IT IS FOR ANYBODY

Humble folk often believe that walking with God is above their heads, or that they may "lose a good time" if they share all their joys with God. What tragic misunderstanding, to regard Him as a killer of happiness! A growing chorus of joyous voices around the world fairly sings that spending their hours with God is the most thrilling joy ever known, and that beside it a baseball game or a horse race is stupid.

RADIANT RELIGION

This game is not a grim duty. No one need play it unless he seeks richer life. It is a delightful privilege. If you forget to play it for minutes or hours or days, do not groan or repent; begin anew with a smile. It is a thrilling joy—don't turn it into a surfaced penance. With God, every minute can be a fresh beginning. Ahead of you lie limitless anticipations. Walt Whitman looked up into the starry skies and fairly shouted:

Away O Soul! hoist instantly the anchor!

*　　*　　*

O daring joy but safe! are they not all the
seas of God?
O farther, farther, farther sail!